POLLY WANTS A LAWYER!

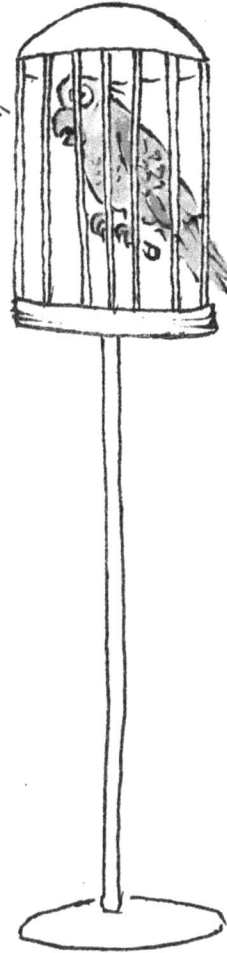

CARTOONS OF
MURDER, MAYHEM & CRIMINAL MISCHIEF
BY NICK DOWNES

HUMORIST
BOOKS

New York

First Printing: 2022

Humorist Books is an imprint of *Weekly Humorist* owned and operated by Humorist Media LLC.

Weekly Humorist is a weekly humor publication, subscribe online at
weeklyhumorist.com

110 Wall Street New York, NY 10005

weeklyhumorist.com - humoristbooks.com - humoristmedia.com

Book design by Marty Dundics

This is a work of fiction. Names, characters, businesses, places, events, locales, and incidents are either the products of the author's imagination or used in a fictitious manner, except in cases when public figures and events are being satirized through fictionalized depictions and/or personality parodies (permitted under Hustler Magazine v. Fallwell, 485 US 46, 108 S.Ct 876, 99 L.E.2d 41 (1988)). Any resemblance to actual persons, living or dead, or actual events is purely coincidental.

Acknowledgement is made to the following publications in which these cartoons originally appeared: *The New Yorker, Playboy, The Spectator, The Oldie, Barron's, The Wall Street Journal, Fantasy & Science Fiction, The American Bystander, The Weekly Standard, National Enquirer* and *Private Eye*.

"In the venerable tradition of Charles Addams and Gahan Wilson, Nick Downes—with this collection of fabulously bizarre, twisted, and sometimes macabre gags—proves himself to be a cartoonist with a deliciously freaky sense of fun."

—Emma Allen,
    Cartoon Editor of *The New Yorker*

To Jeanne

"Just browsing!"

"If a standard capacity magazine holds thirty rounds, and the shooter fires off sixteen, how many bullets are left in the gun?"

10

"These days, Harry and I are just living from forged
check to forged check."

THE CRIMINALLY INSANE GOURMET

NICK DOWNES

"But I'm rambling. How was your day?"

"Okay, so maybe you didn't do it. Surely there's something you have done that you deserve to die for?"

"I'm going to let you off with a beating."

"You guys know any sing-alongs?"

"Ask for just one hand to be lopped off - they expect
you to haggle."

"Now wait a minute - are you calling killing a man for snoring, murder?"

"And finally, may I ask how satisfied you are with the
way I handled your interrogation, today?"

"I'm sorry - I could've sworn it was casual wear Friday."

"Have you got this in a 7 ½?"

"You sound different, Father."

"Luckily for you, Tommy, your dad's alleged mob ties will keep me from giving you the grade you really deserve."

"I will now attempt to get out of jury duty."

"I begged him not to wear that t-shirt."

"Just between you, me and the lamp post, could you
speak more directly into the lamp post?"

"It appears he was caught in the middle of an interpretive dance move."

"What'll stop the little green men?"

"She left me for the guy who stole my identity."

"Whew! You're a tough girl to stalk."

"Is this about my always taking a penny, but never leaving a penny?"

"You're lucky I've given up breaking legs, for Lent."

"He tried to take away Fuzzy Bear."

"Basically, what we've got is the old, boy meets girl, boy loses girl, boy stalks girl, boy kidnaps girl, boy tortures girl, boy…"

"It's me, isn't it?"

"Our first task, of course, is to humanize you to the jury."

"Found him? But I've rented out his room!"

"I thought trench warfare was a thing of the past."

"My name's Aldred, and I'll be your server this evening."

"Before we begin, I ask that you turn off all cell phones."

ANTI-
DESECRATION
PATROL

ERE LIES
HAS KEELM

NICK DOWNES

"I told him his phrase book was hopelessly out of date."

"Just 'cause I fit the description of the guy, doesn't make me the guy."

"Remember, he's got a cat - don't let it out."

"As your probation officer, I must caution you about
this sort of thing."

"Careful - that's my drinking arm."

"The association of homicidal maniacs is going to hear about this!"

"This is an employees only entrance, sir."

"I tried to sleep with the fishes, but they threw me back!"

"You may be interested to know, that at least one of your classmates was concerned enough about his grades to leave an envelope of cash on my desk, yesterday afternoon."

"I assure you, Ms. Matson - this falls within 'generally accepted accounting practice.'"

"Oh, don't look so alarmed - you've seen my flock."

"Hold on, Bob - Isn't contemporary art all about provoking outrage?"

"I didn't say he was an interesting person. I said he
was a person of interest."

"I was quoted out of context."

"He's tunneled out!"

SILENCE STRICTLY ENFORCED.

Nick Downes

"Please, Bob - don't be a hero."

"Elementary, my dear Watson - they're on your head."

"Why can't you show that sort of initiative at getting us a table?"

"Somehow, I assumed Hillcrest Country Club would be free from that sort of thing."

"I warned Eddie about walking past Our Lady Of Little Or No Mercy."

"Honesty is certainly a policy option."

"It's a subpoena!"

"I'm new in town - do you know where one registers as
a sex offender?"

"Visiting hours are over, Mrs. Kornwinkle."

"You're it!"

"Oh, c'mon George - you're not still angry I ratted you out?"

"Maybe that isn't the way it happened, but that's the way it should have happened, and that's the way I'm going to remember it happened."

"This is your lucky day - I'm a crooked cop, on the take."

"I'm referring you to someone more adept at Medicare fraud than I."

"Do you have any more models where the accelerator sticks?"

"I thought embezzling company funds would fulfill me, but,
I just feel empty."

"I want to make you Mrs. Psychotic drifter!"

TRUE CRIME   TRAVEL

OOKS

Nick Downes

"Helen, you look like a grieving widow, in that oufit."

"He died doing what he loved most - shooting it out with the cops."

ACT NORMAL
AND VALIDATE
MY PARKING.

NICK DOWNES

"I can feel my depression lifting."

"This is a great spot for people watching."

"But enough about my problems - you're the one who called 911."

"I'm waiting for someone."

"If I didn't believe so firmly in the separation of church
and state, I'd call the cops."

"We got an unlucky draw."

"You keep out of it, Mac - I'm talking to the dog."

"Don't you hate it when you plant evidence, but forget where?"

"You book an Airbnb, you get what you get, I guess."

"This is my court-appointed lawyer?"

"Oh, Harry - you had so much more to embezzle."

"Maybe you should find another book group."

BREEZY PINES
A GATED COMMUNITY
FOR THE
CRIMINALLY INSANE

Nick Downes

"Kicking an old lady into an oven isn't going to go over well, so we better say she was an evil witch, or something."

"Some people can't be bothered to maintain their yard."

"It's poached salmon, in that it's stolen."

"Bad things happen to people who don't buy my cookies, mister."

"She bridges the hardboiled detective/little old lady
schools of sleuthing."

"He wasn't merry enough."

"He's an obvious flight risk, your honor."

CAUTION
CHILDREN

NICK DOWNES

"Say, Harry - does your wife know you're getting rid of that rug?"

"You can turn off the magic fingers."

"Customers who bought this item also bought speed, crank, smack, blow, and weed."

"Villains!" I shrieked, "dissemble no more! I admit the deed! - Tear up the planks! Here, here! It is the beating of his hideous heart!"

"Look, honey - clowns!"

"George, please - not your humanitarian award!"

"OK, OK - maybe we are lending."

"If he only spent as much time battling evil-doers as
he does guys who make fun of his tights."

ENTERING
PLEASANTVILLE
—
PLEASANTNESS
STRICTLY ENFORCED

Nick Downes

"Can you support my daughter on what you pilfer
from collection plates?"

"They're settling out of court!"

"Stop! Or I'll have a heart attack!"

"Hostage situation, captain - says he didn't get what
he wanted for Christmas."

"I went to a really crummy law school."

"For the plaintiff in this case, your honor, the product's bold assertion: 'easy-opening lid,' was a cruel and vicious lie."

"You never get used to this sort of mayhem."

"That's the third desperate cry for help this month."

"Last chance for one of your pithy *bon mots*."

"It's just like she said it would happen."

"I'm afraid it's merely a forgery of a forgery of one of master forger Han Van Meegeren's bogus Vermeers."

"I'm not saying he isn't a good guard dog, just that his promotion surprised me."

"Sir - is that old lady bothering you?"

"It's rare to see a high-tech criminal doing hard time."

"Found your stress ball, honey!"

"They were after me Lucky Charms."

"Perhaps our boy pulls wings off flies to study aerodynamic equilibrium."

"This must be juvenile court."

"God, I love Christmas."

"At least he'll die surrounded by his family."

"Sorry, Dugan, - you got a stay of execution."

"You were 'bad cop' last time!"

"Have I called at a bad time?"

"I'm the man who shot the man who shot the man who shot the man who shot the man who shot Liberty Valance."

"You set him up, didn't you, Mrs. McGinty? You knew that triple word score would be too much for his heart."

"I wish you wouldn't go through my pockets, Darlene."

"My wallet!"

"That went well, I thought."

"I love what you've done with the basement."

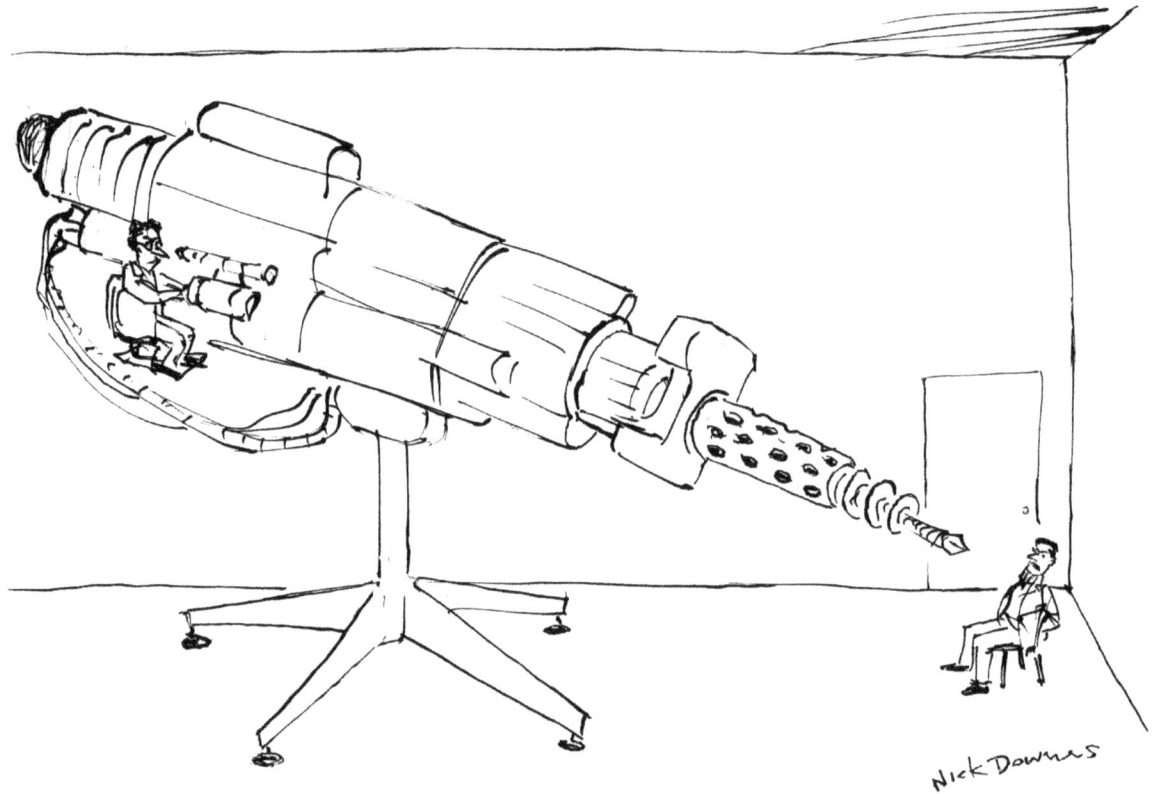

"Take away your thermal infused photon blasting polarized proton anti-matter disintegration gun and you're just a cheap, two bit hood."

TWELVE HAPPY MEN.

Nick Downes resides in Brooklyn, NY. He enjoys watercolors, Puccini, horse racing, and a good cigar.